SPIRIT WISDOM
for Daily Living

clint g. bridges

SPIRIT WISDOM
for Daily Living

clint g. bridges

Edited by Karen Larré, *Truly Alive* Magazine
Cover Art by Diana Massengale, Image Design LLC
Proof Read by Claudette Wilmarth
Author Photo by Jex Wyche Photography
Cover Image "Eye of God" Nebula Hubble Telescope, NASA

SPIRIT WISDOM for Daily Living
Copyright © 2013 by Clint G. Bridges
Revised Edition

Printed in the United States of America
Love Level Publishing
PO Box 476, Bosque, NM 87006
505.889.3545

ISBN-13: 978-0615944319
ISBN-10: 0615944310

Library of Congress Control Number: 2014901359

"The writer who breeds more words than he needs

is making a chore for the reader who reads."

Dr. Seuss

DEDICATION

To my wonderful wife Sheila, for supporting me
in all my endeavors and for her beautiful love that
has sustained me for the past forty-four years.
I love you punkin.'

SPIRIT WISDOM:
A PREFACE

The contents of this book are intended to empower readers and encourage them to take 100% responsibility for the lives they have created; recognizing that while they may seem to be surrounded by uncomfortable circumstances, there were no forces outside of themselves that manifested these conditions.

Therefore, within oneself, one has the personal power to re-create the conditions and circumstances in their life producing a new experience and existence filled with love, peace and harmony.

SPIRIT WISDOM:
AN INTRODUCTION

I have titled this book *Spirit Wisdom For Daily Living* because the ideas and concepts are the principles that have guided me through the last half of my seventy years, in living my life moment to moment — in my own struggle for spiritual perfection. While I wrote the book, it was not composed by me. It came *to* me from a place deep within my Being.

Whether you know it or not, our journey towards spiritual perfection begins the moment we are born. It can be of great benefit to oneself to be an active participant in this endeavor, and the earlier in life one begins the journey, the better.

Please understand that I am not attempting to tell you what to do, what to think or believe. Don't take my word for it. I encourage you to use your imagination… come up with your own ideas and concepts. But, just perhaps these sayings will be the trigger that helps open that door for you.

This is a book of inspirational sayings about living life. These sayings are presented to you each on a single page. A saying may be one line or several. My hope is to bring you, dear reader, into an awakened state of introspection and contemplation about what these ideas mean to you and how they can be used in your life.

continued on following page

There is a little God stuff on these pages…not much, just a little. Don't get scared. Take it from a former atheist; one will not get far on this spiritual journey without a little help from a Higher Power. As a matter of fact, I did not begin my journey until I was thirty-three years old, after having had a personal experience with the Divine. I was in a complete state of surrender. Love and Peace filled my very Being to over flowing. It was then that the *light* came on. I was wide-awake. My journey had begun.

When I was a young boy and had gone out into the world and committed some kind of mischief, (as young boys often do), I always got caught. My dad was a cop, and he always knew everything I did.

I would find myself at home, undergoing the third degree. I never thought I really lied about anything. I would just conveniently omit one or two of the damning details about the adventure I had been on.

I didn't understand I was lying by omission. My mom, or somebody (it was a long time ago and I can't remember exactly who it was) said to me, "Clint, when you tell the truth, you never have to remember what you said."

You see, Truth is timeless, Truth never changes. Truth is the same yesterday, today, and tomorrow. Truth is a concept. As far as I can figure, most concepts have an underlying principle that binds the concept to the outcome.

Hence the saying, "Honesty is the principle behind the concept of Truth."

I have not knowingly plagiarized any material contained in these pages. In cases where I did use known source material, I made the appropriate acknowledgements. If you should find something lacking in terms of acknowledgement, please let me know and I will be happy to add it. On the "sayings" cover page, I have used the term *"Think On These Things."* This is actually the title of a book by J. Krishnamurti that I read a very, very long time ago.

Lastly, I am of the male gender. It matters not; for regardless of our gender expression in this life, we are all made of two parts, male and female, anima and animas. If you are of the feminine expression, please do not take offense at the patriarchal nature of these writings. Just read from your beautiful perspective and enjoy the wisdom in the words.

I bring this material to you in love and light. May it brighten the light that dwells within your Being. Thank you for reading this book. May Love, Peace and Harmony be your companions all the days of your life!

Love and Blessings: Peace and Harmony to you.

Clint

THE SAYINGS

Think On These Things

Can you agree with me, that as units of
Awareness we have a responsibility to explore
the nature of our personal reality and to seek truth?

Have you ever asked yourself these questions?

What am I?
Why am I here?
What am I supposed to be doing, and how am I
supposed to be doing it?

You will have to answer these questions for yourself,
and I hope you make the choice to seek your own
answers.

The question goes beyond whatever society or culture
you may find yourself in. The question goes to the
purpose of life.

As for myself, *Life* is no longer a mystery. *Life* is not
just about the things we do in our daily lives to survive.

Life is about the Mastery of Personal Awareness.
That's all.

What is Spirit?

Isn't Spirit the manifestation of God's energy?

Someone once said that we are Spiritual Beings having a physical experience. Could it be that the purpose of this physical experience is for us to remember our Spiritual Nature?

The whole thrust of living should be to
evolve from a physical being to a Spiritual Being.

Could it be Mother Earth is the proving grounds for Spirits? The Realm where Spirits become Souls?

Do you hunger for truth as I hunger for truth?
Do you thirst for understanding as I thirst for
understanding?

Come with me; together we will become seekers and
finders of wisdom.

Your world is nothing more
than a psychological construct
you have created for yourself,
based on the *agreements* you have
made, *with yourself* and those around you.

This construct and these agreements
have become your belief system.
This is what you believe to be true
about yourself, and the world you live in.

This is your worldview, and your world
view determines the world *you view*.
You have within you, the power to change your
world in the blink of an eye.

We are all together here in this time and place,
on Mother Earth, for one reason…to help one another.
Blessed is the man who understands and accepts *this*
as his truth; for he will be at peace, and his life will
come to him naturally.

Who knows what kindness lurks in the hearts of men?

In the beginning One must lead their Being towards *THAT* which their Heart desires.

Once One has been devoured by Virtue, One no longer needs To-Do; only Follow.

All actions have consequences.

Sometimes you will get more than you think.

Don't forget to think about the unintended consequences.

FOREVER RULES

"Whether you want to know it, and even if you don't accept it, you are completely responsible for the choices you make.

Bad choices will result in bad things happening sooner or later.

Good choices are much less likely to induce bad things to happen, and frequently result in good things happening."

My Uncle Grover. D. Jones 1931-2007

Oh, how I wish that I could have learned this lesson when I was fifteen instead of starting the process in my thirties!

ATTITUDE

There are really only four things we can
control in our life: Our attitude, our actions,
our emotions and our feelings.

Attitude is the mental tool we can use to create our
feelings that produce emotions, which result in actions.

A positive attitude makes one feel good.
That makes for stable emotions that result in right
actions.

How broad and deep is your "Field of Consciousness?"
How far can you *see*? How much can you *hear*?
One does not *see* with their eyes, but rather with
their imagination.

One does not *hear* with their ears, but rather with
their heart.

About 1970, when I was driving north on Shattuck Avenue in Berkeley, California, I saw this bit of graffiti painted on the side of a building:

"God is dog spelled backwards."

I immediately thought to myself; 'Yes, and who *is* man's best friend?'

To reconcile oneself with the concept of God is probably the most important act that any human being could ever do.

Knowledge, Understanding and Wisdom are gifts from our Heavenly Father.

Sometimes Truth can hurt, but it will set you free, if you let it.

I used to think I was an atheist, then I realized *that* was an act of insanity, because it presupposes that this thing we call God *does exist.*

So, I decided to do some discovery, and found for myself, this idea we call "GOD" is in Truth the Source of All That Is…including you and me. I now know SHEHIM as My Heavenly Father.

A man without God, surely must be destined
to wander in the wilderness all the days of his life.

We are All messengers of a Loving God.
Shouldn't we live our lives accordingly?

There are as many Paths as there are people. When we came into this physical world, God embodied in each of us, our own unique Path back home.

And, it came with a round trip ticket. It's up to us to activate the return fare.

How does one find Peace, Harmony and Love?

One does so by seeking that which is already inside one's self. God put *it there* when He created you as an expression of His own Beingness.

All creative endeavors are Divinely
inspired. Understanding this, one should
be certain their words are also Divinely inspired.

Our Heavenly Father has given us free will, and in doing so He also gave us freedom of choice. We can choose to seek Truth in God our creator, or not.

Seeking Truth will always result it choosing the path of Love, Peace and Harmony. When choosing your path, make sure it has *heart*. It is easy to follow the path that has heart because it is the path of Love.

In your Journey upon it, you may find the Love God has for you.

When *that* happens, you will have passed through the Gates of Heaven.

Do you know how our Heavenly
Father measures the love you hold for Him?

It is by the measure of love you
give to yourself and to your neighbor.

Enlightenment needn't be hard or difficult.
A man can go from here to there in the blink of
an eye. Just give up the battle you are having with
yourself…surrender, and let Our Heavenly Father
take over.

These three: Love, Peace, and Happiness come from our Heavenly Father.

Love is *supreme*, followed by peace and happiness.

Use these three as your guides when choosing or changing your path.

Ask yourself…
First, "Am I in Love with this idea?"
Second, "Am I at peace with myself as I contemplate this choice?"
Third, "Can I feel the happiness it will bring now?"

If any one of the three is not present in your heart, flee for your life… for you are about to make a choice that may kill you in the long run.

Truth is a heavy thing, because it forces you to confront your demons and take the righteous path. But, it is also a *light* because the path with heart is always the right choice.

And what do you say to those tempters? The same thing Christ said, "Get thee behind me, Tempter, I'm choosing the righteous path."

Have you ever wondered why it is that in this world in which we co-exist there are wars, murder, famine and all kinds of mayhem?

Could it be because this world (as we now perceive it) is nothing more than the product of man's ego?

When Jesus said, "Be of good cheer, I have overcome the world," do you think it is possible he was saying I have overcome ego? And, in so doing He was demonstrating to all of us that we too could overcome *our own egos?*

Do the wheels of evolution ever cease turning?
I think not.

Divine Mind is always expanding...
consciousness forever birthing new awareness.

I go on a need to know basis: I figure if I need to know, HE will tell me.

The nature of existence is *Being*.

Most people believe that life
happens to them from the outside *in*.
Those who understand, know that
worlds are created from the inside *out*.

People say knowledge is power.
The Good Book says,
Understanding is Wisdom.
I will choose the latter.

Your story is about the evolution of your Mind
as it soars through Eternity on the wings of your Spirit.

If you were the last person in existence, you could fire the "Big Bang" all over again…for you *are* ALL THAT IS.

Heart is the Throne of Love.

Mind is the Seat of Wisdom.

Awareness is <u>the</u> Realm of Being.

Love has no expectation…
therefore Love needs no object.

Heaven is not a place,
It is a state of mind.
If you have not found *It*,
change your way of thinking,
and you will find you are already there

Being Loved gives you Humility.
Loving someone gives you Compassion.

There are two ways to live;
from the mind or from the heart.
The wise one will always choose
the path that is of the heart.

Lost in time and space…drawn like
a moth to light…I am pulled towards my
irresistible source. *THAT*, which *is* Truth. The *One*.

First, be glad.

Your Joy will find you, and

carry you to the doorsteps of Bliss.

We all rise in the morning
and don our costume for the day. Then
some of us put on our masks. Don't do that. Do
not be afraid to be the "real" you. You are magnificent!

Life is kind of like a science project
where we learn the art of living. Or one
could say; living is kind of like an art project
where we learn the science of life.

Happiness requires no effort or doing
for it is our natural state of *Being*. If you're
not happy, examine your thoughts and cast out
those that steal your joy. They are of no use to you.

You don't need a Guru.

You are your own best Guru. You came fully equipped.

Your teacher is built in. Learn to listen; learn to *hear* that still small voice…learn to *follow* what you hear.

Thoughts are like musical notes...they are out there and eventually find their way into the musician's mind. He chooses this one, rejects that one, rearranges them, and makes beautiful music.

Your thoughts are like musical notes. Choose your thoughts with understanding and wisdom. You will create a beautiful life.

Know this to be true:

When you harm another, you harm yourself.

Be kind…not only to others, but also to
yourself, for kindness is the beginning of Love.
First Love yourself, and you will have Love to give.

There is no duality in Truth.

What you think about me does not matter
to me; for I know what I think about myself, and
that is not based on appearances. I understand that
what you think about me is based on what you think
about yourself.

An eternity of Karma can be
forgiven in a moment of Grace.

You can be your own best friend, or
your own worst enemy. The choice is yours.

Incorruptibility is the
principle behind the Concept of Virtue.

Light dwells in Light. There is no Light in darkness.

If a man dwells in darkness and does not know he is in darkness, then he *is* darkness.

Light is consciousness and can only
express Itself; and will always manifest
Itself according to the concept it holds of Itself.

Humility is the principle
behind the Concept of Compassion.

Heading west on Central Avenue in Albuquerque, New Mexico, I saw this bit of graffiti on the side of a building:

"If you want to change the world, change yourself."

My first thought was: 'If you want to make the world a better place, become a better person.'

Honesty is the principle behind the Concept of Truth.

When adverse events happen in your life, and
they most certainly will, do not curse them for they
are Blessings in disguise. They are the elements you have
created in your life. They are to be used as your guides to
move you away from that which you dislike; towards
that which you love.

How can you recognize someone who is filled
with *Light?*
That person is filled with Joy.

Life is an expression of awareness.

Are you *awake?*

This world is the material that
Spiritual symbols are made from.

"Hello...hello...
Is there any body in there?
Is there any body home?"

PINK FLOYD

WAKE UP!

MAKE YOURSELF ALIVE!

Here's an exercise and a question for you:

"Open your eyes and look within.
Are you satisfied with the life you're livin"?

BOB MARLEY

If you're not satisfied, just make a shift in your thinking.
If you are satisfied you've probably already made
the shift.

People – Wake up! Turn on your Light.

The switch is in your Heart. The power is in your Mind.

Is your Light switch on, or is it off?

Our answers lay waiting to be found in the silence.

Integrity is the principle behind the Concept of Ethics.

Life is a process. It's not meant to be a
beginning and an end. It's meant to be a beginning,
and a beginning. Both beginnings are for *this time
and place.*

It is the movement from a physical being to a *Spiritual
Being.*

It does not matter what it is. One always has
to do the right thing, no matter what the cost. The
cost for doing the wrong thing will always be greater.

What is "Enlightened Self Interest?"

It means that if *it* is not as equally as good
for you, as it is for me, it won't work. Don't do it!

By our own volition, bring we forth
our fruits. You would not want to eat a bitter
fruit; but rather that which is sweet to the senses.

"Sane people love Truth. Sober people <u>live</u> Truth."

MY WIFE, SHEILA

"Nothing is either good or bad; thinking makes it so."

SHAKESPEARE

"Out beyond the ideas of right and wrong, there is a field. I will meet you there."

RUMI

"A wise person does not associate with a fool. The wise person is perfect in all wisdom, but to the fool, good and evil are one and the same."

JESUS THE CHRIST TO HIS DISCIPLES

Which of the three is correct in their observation?

My definition of a Good thought:

A good thought promotes Life.
A good thought produces Harmony.
A good thought prospers Love.

If a thought does not do these three things, it is
of no use. Rid yourself of it as quickly as possible.

There are three forces at work in this world.

The first force creates life and provides an environment for life to prosper.

The second force does it's best to destroy all that the first force does.

The third force does all it can do to rescue all that the first force does from the second force.

I will not allow my emotions and feelings to
be bound by things over which I have no control.

I understand that in my life, the only thing I have
complete control over, is my attitude, emotions, and
feelings.

Understanding is not _just_ an act
of kindness towards one another.

It's also an act of kindness towards oneself,
and one of the best gifts you can give to yourself.

Is there a difference between giving and receiving?
I think not. For the gift received is an act of giving.

Did you know that you are being
bombarded with Blessings – right now?

They are coming at you like arrows of
Love from the outer space of your mind.

They are bubbling up inside of
you like an eternal spring of life.

All you need to do is take down your
walls, and allow yourself to receive them.

If you go with your heart instead of your head,
you may find fewer disappointments in your life.

Life is always in the process
of becoming more than what it is.

Consciousness is always expanding…awareness
is always growing…and mind is always evolving.

If you think you see evil in the world,
what should you do? You should send it love.

Most of us had our hearts broken when we
were little children, and that's when the Untruth began.

Are you still living the Untruth?

One of the most important practices we can learn to master is the art of being here; with all of our awareness focused in the present moment.

It is in this state of Being that one has access to their personal power.

We may divide the mind however we choose:
Conscious, un-conscious, sub-conscious,
super-conscious or cosmic-conscious…but in the end,
we really have One Awareness and *its* performance is
solely determined by the clarity of our Intent.

The first step towards Happiness is simply Gladness.

This is the way awareness works:
First it forgets, and then it remembers.

It is one thing to know something intellectually...in your mind.

It is entirely another thing to experience that same knowing in your heart, where it's transformed into understanding and wisdom.

The first changes nothing. The latter creates anew every atom in your body.

Emotion is the connective tissue between mind and heart...for it is one's emotion that transports what the mind knows *into the heart.*

This is how knowledge becomes understanding and wisdom.

Our sense of separateness comes from the divide between our hearts and our minds.

When the heart and mind are one, we are one within ourselves, and one with All That Is.

Life is an expression of awareness.

Are you *awake?*

We are co-creators with the
Supernatural. Together we create the natural.

It is our nature to create, and we do it so naturally
and easily that we don't even realize that we are doing *it*.

When you speak with words of
Love, Love will come back to you.
I promise. Sooner or later it will come
back to you, some times in unexpected ways.

It's a funny thing about fulfillment:
it happens before you even know it!

It seems to me, that sometimes the road to perfection is a matter of choosing the lesser of two evils.

Peacefulness of itself, by its
own nature, is a Spiritual quality.

Joy is equal.

When walking down a path in shoes and seeing a pebble in the way, could you be the kind of person that stoops down and removes it, for the person following behind you may be barefoot?

You'll see it when you believe it.

There are two forces at work in the
world…Life and Death, Being and Non-Being.
Choose wisely.

There are no innocent bystanders.
There are no victims. There are only Creators
standing amidst their chaos...learning how to create.

From out of nothing comes chaos...then
confusion, followed by reason, knowledge,
understanding, wisdom, order and *life*.

Political solutions have very little to offer mankind. The only True and lasting solutions are Spiritual in nature.

This life is both a physical and a Spiritual event.

"Smile! You're on God's camera."

My Mom/Grandma

"If you can't be thankful for the things you have,
be thankful for the things you escaped."

MY MOM/GRANDMA

Do not be hasty to judge. Rather, be open to all things, but quick to discriminate...choosing only that which expands your capacity to give and receive Love.

If there is an objective purpose
to this life, and I believe there is, *It*
surely must be to become fully *"Humanized."*

Your personal power resides within your
words, so be careful what you say to yourself.

To love is our natural way
of being. To hate is unnatural.

Be impeccable in all that you do.
If you always do your best, you will never look back
on your life and say to yourself, "I could have
done better."

By the fruits of your actions you shall
live, and either suffer or rejoice in your life.

Out of the kindness of his heart
does a man bring forth the good treasure.

I am so happy and glad to be alive today.

I am like a little child…so full of joy and
excitement…wondering what new discoveries
this new day will bring forth for my delight!

"A lot of people seem to think that they are special. What they need to understand is, _so is everyone else!_"

MY SISTER JANE MARIE

Awareness has three aspects: female, male and female and male as *one*.

The third is neither male nor female, but is greater than the sum of the two. *It* represents the oneness of mind, and is one with Spirit.

Here I am, sitting in this moment, waiting with
awe and wonder for the next moment to unfold.

"This is a new moment."

LOUISE HAY

"After we're gone from this world, all that remains is the good we've done...and it goes on and on and on and on."

MY GRANDMA

"Things don't change. You change your way of thinking. That's all."

DON JUAN MATUS

When we change our way of thinking, we change our worldview. When we change our worldview, we change the world we view.

Mind is the tool that awareness uses to focus Its self.

I have requested from Universe two guides: The Father of Truth for my Mind and The Teacher of Righteousness for my Heart

Are we aware that our egos posses us most of the time? It should be the other way around.

Why do I have these momentary lapses of sanity… where I fall back into the clutches of ego?

Is it possible to have a sense of ones' self with out ego?

Your ego is not your true nature.

Seek and find your true nature; you will

find yourself and become that which you truly are.

God is trapped inside of us…yearning to
be set free; but our egos will not allow it.

Ego is always seeking self-validation from other egos. Why? Because, deep down it knows *that* it's full of horseshit.

I will let my Heavenly Father be my validator.

(ok, you can change it to horse manure)

Behind the veil of ego lay the true nature of humankind.
It is Loving Spirit.

One day, I became aware that my ego was suffering the effects from one or more of the Seven Deadly Sins. (I prefer Seven Deadly Ignorances.)

What can I do, I ask?
HE answered and said, "Feed your ego from the Spirit of Meekness."

How does one do that you may ask?

I began to watch my ego, and provide instruction.
I began to show my ego the way, by saying to it:

Do this, not that.
Say this, not that.
Think this, not that.
Feel this, not that.
Act this way, not that way.

Now, I am getting well.

Seek not to be one with all that is around you, but rather seek to be one with the in-dwelling Holy Spirit. When you find oneness within yourself the other will follow.

The secret to Oneness is to have a Spirit of meekness.

We should be kind to one another,

because kindness is the beginning of Love.

Joy is not found in what happens to you,
but rather how you react to what happens to you.

The amount of joy you find in your life is not
determined so much by what you get, but by how you
react to what you get.

Living life is about doing the thing that you want
to do, *and* doing the thing that you don't want to do.

"You have to change your heart to change."

BOB DYLAN

"You know it's possible to become so defiled in this world that your own father and mother will abandon you, and if that happens, God will always believe in your ability to mend your ways."

BOB DYLAN

From the moment we are born, our
own death begins to stalk us…waiting,
waiting for us to make the wrong move.

We're here today and gone tomorrow. If you want to have a tomorrow, you had better think about what you do today.

Take death as an advisor.

Do not delay until tomorrow
those things that you should do today!

Your tomorrow might not arrive.

Some say you can't avoid the taxman and death.

I am more afraid of the taxman than death.
I think most people are afraid of confronting their own death.

How does one confront death?
By living your life with Impeccability and Integrity.

When things happen in life, don't get your tail feathers in a tizzy. Its just life: something to observe. That's all.

If you want a miracle, expect one.

When you look at people, what you see on the outside is of very little importance. It's what's on the inside that matters, and to discover *that* you need to get acquainted with them.

There are three things I want to understand:

1. The function of consciousness.
2. The nature of awareness.
3. The structure of mind.

I have not yet received that wisdom, but I will.

If there is a reward for doing the right thing, it is this: One does not suffer the consequences for doing the wrong thing.

The right thing is simply and always the wisest choice.

Life does not taste of death.

Most people only think about what's in it
for me. A better way, is what's in it for us.

Mind is a function of Awareness.

When your Heart is in alignment
with your Intent, *All* things are possible.

The way you feel about a person will either
bring out the worst, or the best of your Being.

"*You can change people by*
changing your attitude towards them."

UNKNOWN

The way to change a negative situation into a positive one is to continually manifest your inherent positive nature into the situation.

Eventually, the situation will change from one of darkness to one of *light*.

It is thoughts of Love and Peace that will bring Joy and Harmony to your Being. And that will result in a healthy body and a sound mind.

Thoughts of hatred, anger, fear and jealousy will result in disease and confusion.

Everyone has (in this lifetime) the opportunity to clear all karma and get off the Wheel of Life and Death.

Heaven is a land of Love and Peace.

How does one enter there into?

Bring some Love and Peace.

A little joy will go a long way too.

Be careful. Pause and think
before you speak, words *are* deeds.

"If you have to knock on Heaven's door, you are in the wrong neighborhood."

MY LIFE PARTNER, SHEILA

Life is not so much about what you get, as it is to *how you react* to it. Because how you react will *be what you create* in your life.

If you are confronted by anger in a situation and you react with anger, you *have just created anger* in your life. On the other hand, when you react with passivity, the anger is nullified and has no effect.

Always…be at peace in *all ways.*

Just like eating an apple one bite at a time, we can change our lives by changing one belief at a time.

All things begin as an idea in your mind. *It is your imagination at work.* Be careful the things you imagine, for they will become manifest in your life.

Compassion is probably the most important word in the human language. Show yourself a little mercy, and have compassion for yourself. Do not be critical of yourself; be understanding towards yourself.

HE made you *perfect*.

I have heard it said that the eyes are the window
to the soul.

We are all born with a *light* in our eyes. Even if with the
passage of time it has dimmed, or we no longer can see
it, it remains...for it is the light of our Spirit, and can be
rekindled at any time.

Heart is the Throne of Love

Mind is the Seat of Wisdom

Awareness is <u>the</u> Realm of Being.

What is the opposite of Love? If you say hate, you are mistaken in your perception. The correct answer is fear. Hate is just a by-product of fear.

We tend to hate that which we do not understand and are fearful of.

Be not afraid. Seek understanding and you will find Love.

Do not become discouraged by the
world you see around yourself; rather,
become a beacon of *light* in a sea of darkness.

When knowledge becomes understanding, wisdom has arrived. You have become the tiller of your ship.

Do you have a dream in your heart? Pursue it until it becomes manifest in your life. Do everything in your power to bring it forth. Allow nothing to stop you. This is the reason you are here – now – in this time and place.

Desire is not the cause of suffering.
It is ignorance of God, which causes
error of thought and suffering follows.
Desire is the emotion that fires imagination.
Imagination births the inspiration that mind
uses to expand consciousness, bringing *light* to that
which was in darkness. My only desire
is to be one with the Mind of Christ.

We live in a world of duality, night and day,
light and darkness, hot and cold, male and female.
Let us consider female and male, one is no less and no
more than the other. For together as equals, they induce
the necessary contrast for an atmosphere that creates
harmony and growth.

Every time I ask Mind a question,
the answer takes me to the next level.

I AM awake
I AM consciousness,
I AM awareness,
I AM aware,
I AM mind,
I AM Being,
I AM <u>that</u> I AM.

There is no Darkness in Light.

There is no Light in Darkness.

Darkness cannot enter into Light.

But Light can enter into Darkness,

and *it* will, especially when invited.

We all are bound to encounter
rejection in life…maybe a lot. That's life.

Learn to use rejection as a steppingstone
for bringing out the best in yourself.

When I awoke this morning, I was in such a state of Samadhi, tears rolling freely down my checks. Every thought that comes into my mind is an affirmation of His Love for each one of us.

My body creaks and groans under the mighty weight of His Love, but I feel no heaviness at all.

GROW YOUR GARDEN

Life is never greener on the other side of the highway.

In fact, many creatures lose their lives trying to get to what appears to be greener pastures across the fence.

A wise man will make a stand where he is. He will sow his seeds and plant his garden. He feeds it, cares for it, and nurtures it with tender loving mercies. It will flourish and become a thing of living beauty.

He regards it as a precious work of art, and it will become a personal Garden of Eden to him.

THE ROOM FULL OF LOVE

The next time you find yourself in a room full people, (it might be a restaurant, church, or a meeting), you may make a wonderful discovery, if you think of it this way:

Each person in that room either has someone that loves them, or has someone they love. You are in a "Room Full of Love."

Take a moment to reflect on what you see. Can you feel it? "The Room Full of Love?"

WORDS HAVE POWER

Most of us throw our words around with out any thought to the power we are wielding. Words have the power to start a war, or bring about peace.

If you are not careful, words can be like an atomic bomb blowing up in your face.

Words can inflict hurt and pain. Words can utterly destroy that to which they are directed towards…or they can be a soothing balm of tender mercies that bring comfort – healing mental and emotional wounds, promoting life and love.

THE PATH TO WISDOM

First ask a question…any question — it doesn't matter.
HE will answer. Listen very, very closely to the answer.

If you don't understand the answer, ask the question
again in a different way. Repeat the process until
you *understand the answer.* You have now acquired
knowledge with understanding…you're on the Path to
Wisdom. Go ahead. Ask another question!

Footnote: In order for this technique to work one must
first completely assume personal responsibility for every
thing that happens in their life.

IE: I created this situation, event, circumstance etc.
What can I learn?

BECOMING HUMAN

There is a Beast that roams through the wilderness of this world, infecting the minds of Homo Sapiens. It spews the emotional poisons of fear, hate, jealousy, envy, greed, pride, lust, hypocrisy, sloth and all manner of evil imaginings, and the mental defect of ignorance. Those consumed are they who wither and die in darkness.

All is not lost…for there is a Being that dwells in the hearts of mankind who brings forth the emotional fruits of love, joy, compassion, humility, charity, faith, and self-mastery. Those in touch with this Being are those who live in *light* and have found *life*.

I think this is what the ancient ones called "the battle between the Sons of Light and the sons of darkness."

I AM THAT I AM

What am I?

What are you?

What are we?

We are not the body.

We are not the ego. So, what are we?

If you were fortunate when you were born,
your family gathered around to witness the newly
arrived babe, unspoiled and untouched by the world…
in all *its* purity and innocence. Someone may have made
the remark, "this is as close as we ever get to seeing God
in this world." This *is* what I am: *THAT*. And, so are you
and everyone else!

So, this is what we do: We awaken and return to *THAT*.

BEGINNINGS

There's nothing new under the Son…
nothing left to do that's not already done…
no new stories to be told that were not spoken
way back in the days of old.

No new songs to sing that haven't already been sung…
we're just here, on the threshing room floor, where the
harvester separates the chafe from the wheat; the refiner,
the dross from the gold…just outside heaven's door.

THE RIDE

I am seated in my Chariot.
I care not where or whence
it goes, for I have no fear.
I trust Spirit, and let *It* carry
me where it will. My only duty,
is to enjoy the ride and the view.

HEART

What a truly wonderfully, magical and interesting word it is.

HEART…the Main Organ of Sense.
HEART…the Throne of Love.
If you have an <u>EAR</u> to <u>HEAR</u>
<u>HE</u> will show you the science of life.
<u>HE</u> will teach you the <u>ART</u> of living.

HEART…the Seat of the Sixth Sense.

WHAT'S IN A CONCEPT?
EVERYTHING. THAT'S ALL.

The concept you hold about yourself in your mind is all of your beliefs rolled up into one idea. You. You are that concept whatever it may be, and it is the reality you are experiencing in your life in this world right now! Be it rich man, beggar man, happy man or sad man.

If a man believes he is poor he may be a beggar standing on the corner looking for a handout. That is his concept of himself. It has hardened into his reality, and the riches of his mind have become lost to him.

If a women is battered and she believes that she deserves to be mistreated and abused and that she is powerless to do any thing about it, that is her concept of herself, and therefore, that is her reality.

If a man behaves like a criminal and believes there is no other way to survive other than by violating others in society that is his concept of himself, and consequently it has become that person's reality.

On the other hand, a man may be a physicist who holds the concept that by using his intelligence he can understand the working of the universe and the nature of physical reality. Because that man holds a higher concept of himself, the world reveals an Einstein or a Hubble.

continued on following page

If you have a desire to improve your lot in life, it's easy. All you need to do is change the concept you hold about yourself to a higher concept. When you have become that concept of yourself, and you will, seek still a higher concept of yourself. You will also become that.

As for myself, the highest concept I can see is this: God made me. He made me in His own image and likeness. I have been perfected in God's Love. I am a loving Human Being, and that is the energy that guides my behavior and creates the world I live in.

I believe this is true for myself, and intuitively, I understand that His wisdom flows to all of us, because the same God made each and every one of us.

EGO

We all have one.
What is it?
Why do we have one?
Where does it come from?

In the beginning, new life is helpless…completely dependent on those in its environment for care and nurturing. As a part of the "Life Process," life itself provides the survival mechanism we know as Ego. Ego begins as a caretaker; its purpose to make certain we receive from our environment that which we need to grow and survive. Alas, ego is the guardian that turns into the guard.

As we develop physically and mentally from infancy to adulthood, acquiring the ability to feed and clothe ourselves… evolving our inner sense of self; our ego is also developing. By this time, the ego is completing its move from caretaker and guardian to guard.

The ego knows that its worldview is an illusion that has been created around its emotional reaction to the events and people in its environment. Perhaps we grew up poor or rich. Perhaps someone said we were stupid or ugly, smart or pretty. It doesn't matter. The ego has accepted and agreed with such ideas as truth and made them a part of its belief system. Therefore, we have become subject to that. We are not subject to anything; we should not believe anything our ego tells us is true. Ego is a false self. Learn to listen.

continued on following page

We are not our ego. We are THAT which we were when we were born, before ego. We are the True and Eternal Godhead!

And so, we come to another "Life Process." We awaken to the tyranny of the ego.

And I say to my ego, 'Old friend, you have served me well and I love you for it. Now, come with me, leave behind the trials of illusion and falsehood. Fear no longer; for I will take care of you as you have taken care of me. I will show you the pathways to Truth and teach you that which is righteous. Together we will become as one and enter into the wellspring of *Life*.'

Upon being asked when they would enter into the Kingdom of Heaven, by his disciples, I think this is what Jesus meant when he replied, "When the two are one, and the outside is like the inside, and the inside is like the outside, then you will enter into Kingdom of Heaven."

THE GRACE OF GOD

On my morning drive to work every day, there is a stoplight where I get off the freeway. Very frequently, there stands a panhandler on the corner begging for a hand out.

My reaction in the past has been to judge this person as an alcoholic, drug addict, lazy bum, or just a free loader.

My mode of action was to pretend that he wasn't there, and to avoid eye contact at all cost.

On this particular morning, I suddenly had the following thought come into my heart and mind: (It was as if, God said to me, "be grateful for the panhandler standing on the corner when you pull up to the stoplight, for he makes it possible for you to perform a simple act of kindness and charity.")

I very happily pulled out a couple of bucks and handed them over. From now on, I will make sure that I always have a few dollars in my pocket for just such an occasion.

I look forward to the day when my affluence will permit me to pass along a five dollar bill instead of a couple of ones… perhaps even a ten spot, or more.

Judge not, lest you be judged yourself.

But for the Grace of God, there go I.

You are *such a Blessing.*

My perfect world could not be if you were not in it.

"I will not work for fame or wealth,
for what I owe cannot matter much.
It's what I am that counts."

AUTHOR UNKNOWN

T H E   E N D

ACKNOWLEDGEMENTS

To my mom Lois and my step-dad Seth: Thank you for teaching me to always do the right thing, and to always lend a hand to those in need. I appreciate you for making me go to church when I was a youngster. You said that I should learn about God so I could make up my own mind. I love you dearly.

To my sisters: I am grateful Claudette, for your proof reading skills and Jeanne for your computer skills; as well as both of you putting up with me when we were growing up. I would have disowned me if I were either of you.

To my dear friend Karen Larre: Without your encouragement and excellent editing skills, this book may never have come to print. Love and Blessings to you.

"Happy surprises are coming my way." Karen Larré.

To Diana Massengale for transforming my manuscript into the beautiful work of art you are holding in your hands. Diana you are such a Blessing!

MY BIO

I was told that I needed to tell my readers why I have the credentials to write this book. I don't really have a burning desire to do so. I'm a private person...almost a recluse, but I do love people. One can learn a lot about oneself by watching and studying people.

Some cultures believe that the world is a mirror and all you ever really see is your own reflection coming back to you. Therefore, if you see something in another that you don't like, you can only see it because the same trait dwells in your own being. The same God made us all.

I've been a drunkard and a dope addict. I've broken just about all of societies rules and made just about every dumb ass mistake that a man could make. When I was a kid they called me a rebel. After I was honorably discharged from the Marine Corps, I considered myself an outlaw — eventually evolving into what I considered to be a maverick. I was unwilling to live by the phony baloney egocentric rules of hypocritical society. I now understand that all I really ever was (and truly am) is a Free Spirit.

I don't have any special degrees or fancy titles. Just a high school diploma, and I did graduate from the "school of hard knocks." I guess the only credentials I have is that I'm seventy years old and I've been married to the same woman for the past forty-four years. I hope to God I've learned something worthwhile about this life along the way. I am still amazed when I wake up in the morning and there she is by my side. It blows my mind!

continued on following page

You can please some of the people some of the time, but you can't please all of the people all of the time, so don't try. I don't know who said that, but the only person you need to worry about pleasing is yourself. Always be true to yourself no matter what.

It matters not whether you agree with me or not or even like me. I don't need you to like or love me. I already love myself. It's your choice to make.

You can call me clint.

This book was written to empower you to believe in yourself! I appreciate and welcome your questions and comments
clintgbridges@gmail.com

Made in the USA
Charleston, SC
10 March 2014